THE LAZY DOG OWNERS TEN-MINUTE TRAINING PLAN

Published by
Elite Publishing Academy
www.elitepublishingacademy.co.uk

First Edition published 2020

Printed and bound in Great Britain by
Elite Publishing Academy

A catalogue record for this book
is available from The British Library

ISBN 978-1-912713-58-5

Contents

Introduction

How the 'Ten Minute' Training plan will change your life

Do you struggle to exercise your dog off lead at the beach because he runs off the second he sees another dog?

I hear you!

Is your dog so excited when you take him for a walk you end up being pulled all the way to the park?

That was me!

Can't leave your dog home alone because he barks incessantly and upsets your neighbours, or chews the house to pieces?

Me too. I've been there; bought the T-shirt and my dog chewed that up too!

Owning a dog can be one of the most rewarding things you can ever do in your life. But if you don't understand your dog and fail to give him what he actually needs to be fulfilled as a dog, then it can also be stressful, upsetting, expensive, depressing and leave you feeling helpless as to how to change his annoying behaviours.

It can get worse than just having an 'embarrassing dog'.

Did you know 50% of dogs in rescue centres were given up by their owners between 5 months and 3 years of age (i.e. once they stopped being cute).

This means many perfectly healthy dogs are put into a rescue, not because of aggression, but just because the owner either couldn't handle the dog or leave the dog home alone.

I don't think any of those owners got a dog thinking one day they would get rid of it, but it can and does happen.

It doesn't have to be that way.

The easier a dog is to look after the greater the chance you will want to keep him forever and the more enjoyable it will be to live with him. You don't have to have a dog that chews your belongings, barks at the window and doesn't come back to you in the park.

Instead, you can have a dog that looks to you as his true best friend rather than just 'the person who feeds me twice a day.'

I get it though. You are busy, and simply don't have the time to watch Crufts once a year, or read a dog training book, never mind attend a series of training classes.

The truth is though, you don't need to.

Actually, that's not true. If your dog has serious behavioural issues and you are worried about *his* safety, *your* safety, *or* the safety of anyone in your community your dog might injure, then you should definitely seek the help of a professional behaviourist, NOW.

But, if your dog is just a bit naughty on walks, if he turns 'stone deaf' when you are calling him back, and if he's your best friend when you are cuddling him on the couch but outside he treats you like a leper with B.O. then you need to implement the 'ten minute' training tips I'm about to share with you in this book.

The perfect dog requires a perfect (and easy to follow) plan

We all dream of owning the perfect dog that we love and who loves us in return, right?

Of course we do. Well, dreaming about it will only get you so far, and it takes action to turn the dream of owning a perfect dog into reality.

Think about the things that you have achieved in your life. If you have ever passed your driving test, paid for a holiday, run a 10K, launched a business, graduated or got a job then you have achieved that by TAKING ACTION.

Yes I know you lead a busy life, I do too!

Most of us work which takes up a lot of our day. Then there's the school run, daily cooking, shopping and cleaning chores. Add into that some family time, and that's before we make any time for any hobbies.

The trick for a busy pet dog owner like you is to find the time to exercise your dog in your already busy, hectic, and stressful life.

Failure to fix that problem means you'll have an under-exercised, under-stimulated, and unfulfilled dog who is bored, destructive and difficult to control.

You need to *and* should make time to do stuff with your pet because once you do, then life with your dog will be a whole lot easier.

If any of the problems and scenarios I have described so far sound familiar to you, then keep reading, because the 'lazy dog trainer' is about to share the three key activities I put into practice every day with my own and my clients' dogs.

Once you discover these simple dog training 'life-hacks', then life with your dog will become as easy as, well…. a walk in the park.

I'll explain more why this is the 'lazy dog owners guide' in just a moment, but before I dive into my story, and why this short book is different to anything else you've ever read, let me lay on the line what's at stake here, and what you need to bring to the party.

How to get what you <u>want</u> by giving your dog what he <u>needs</u>

Believe it or not, your dog is a finely tuned, stealthy, manipulative, sofa seeking machine.

Yes, I'm talking about that four-legged stink ball lying next to you on the couch.

It's taken 'Canis Familiaris', the common house dog, tens of thousands of years to worm his way into our hearts and homes.

Your dogs' great, great, great (great X gazillion) grandfather started this journey hanging around the edge of Ugg the caveman's hearth. He would steal or be given scraps, and gradually, man and dog became great friends.

The dog always had a job like guarding or hunting, and he was always rewarded with companionship and food.

A dog's role changed over the intervening years. And as we became more civilised so the jobs our dogs do become more refined and specialised.

This resulted in the myriad of mutts we have today. From your high performance, like your Vizslas, Pointers and Cocker Spaniels, to your tenacious Border Terriers. There's a dog for every occasion and occupation.

Dogs were essentially bred to do a certain type of job. So, we have gun dogs, herding dogs, water dogs, drugs detection dogs, assistance dogs, racing dogs and lapdogs. If man could find a way to harness a dog's natural skills to make a 'job' easier, then that is what he did.

Dogs were busy and happy, and man enjoyed help with activities and the friendship that only dogs can give.

Some dogs are still in full 'employment' now, but many others are still 'pre-programmed' to do the job they were originally bred to do, but they have no outlet for their natural drive to hunt, chase, play, dig and search.

Now they are dogs on the dole.

Unemployed sofa surfing housebound hounds, out of work, and often in trouble.

Most dogs that are accused of being 'bad dogs' are, in fact, just bored mutts who were simply looking for some kind of 'work' to do that makes them feel like a dog again.

We silly humans thought we could buy their love, and placate their drive to work with fancy bowls, clothes and other pointless shit they don't need.

But we were wrong.

That's why we have more pet professionals, dog training books, podcasts and YouTube videos, plus doggy day-care centres, toys, treats and luxury apparel available than ever before… yet, our rescue centres are full to bursting with dogs who simply weren't given what they need.

So, if you want to do right by your dog, then please understand you can't buy him off with *stuff.*

He doesn't necessarily need to go herding sheep, flushing pheasants or chasing rats down holes, but if you are struggling to control him because his pent-up energy is turning him into a pest, then that's a sure-fire sign your dog does need more than just a walk around the block.

And if you dream of having an easy to control canine who follows you around the park like the Pied Piper, then this book holds the key to your success.

Without action, dreams rarely come true, and while you may love him very much, giving just affection and cuddles are not really going to be enough to satisfy your dog.

Trust me, I know - I've owned dogs for over 20 years.

I wish I knew back then what I do now!

So who on earth am I to tell you about dogs? Well, here is my story.

My big fat dog training mistake

In 2011, I left my job of 10 years as a sales rep for a FTSE 100 company. It was an enjoyable enough job, and it paid the bills, but I didn't really want to do it for another 20-plus years. Call it a midlife crisis if you want, but I'd had enough and wanted to do something else. I also knew I definitely didn't just want to dive into a similar job in sales, so what was I to do?

Well, I'd had enough of working indoors, so a job with access to fresh air was a must. My main interest at that time was dogs. I had this germ of an idea to start my own business where I could combine the two, and people always say you should find a business doing something you love, don't they? But still, I was a little afraid of telling Beth and the kids that I wanted to start a dog-walking business in the middle of a recession.

In my spare time, I had been walking some of the dogs that were awaiting adoption at my local rescue, and it was around then that we adopted our Dogue de Bordeaux, Barry.

Now don't start giggling, because the name suits him! Getting an 18-month-old rescue dog came with some challenges, and I had been reading a lot of books about dog training to give me the tools to help Barry settle in.

When Barry came into our lives, he was a big ginger ball of energy. This is often the case with rescue dogs, and one of the main reasons dogs are given up is because they don't get enough exercise, and they can then become unruly and destructive. The Dogue de Bordeaux is not a breed that is known to be high energy, or so we were told. So to get rid of the pent-up energy Barry had, I did lots of exercise with him. We walked a lot. We jogged together too. We cycled, again with him jogging alongside rather than on a tandem! I bought him a doggy backpack too, which he really enjoyed wearing, and he used to pull much less when he wore it.

So with some rather patchy success with exercising and training Barry under my belt, and my love of being outside in sun, sleet, hail, and snow, I convinced myself, and then Beth and the kids, that I would start my own dog-walking business. Well, a dog-walking business with a difference. I wanted to offer more for dog owners than just a walk around the block. I didn't know much, but I knew that dogs that had some good exercise every day would generally be better behaved and sleep better. I hoped there would be people like me who put a value on a service that offered high-energy adventures for dogs. So that's what I did.

In Sunderland, we are blessed to be a 10-minute drive away from beautiful beaches, parks, woods, and plenty of countryside. So I used to pick up my clients' dogs, and we would have an adventure somewhere different every day. We soon got into a routine of hiking for an hour or so, and then I would let the dogs off lead to have a sniff and a toilet break. But this little break wasn't so chilled out for me.

When the dogs were off lead and had finished their sniffing, some of them would start to play together. They seemed to enjoy this and, I will be honest, I didn't mind too much either, as it gave me a chance to get my breath back. However, the playing quite quickly became a problem, and I was finding it really difficult to get the dogs back on lead again. The downtime had become party time for them. They were having such fun playing together, and they needed me less and less. I was finding it more difficult to get them to listen to me at all, even when I shouted at them. This escalated to the point where I didn't want to let them off lead at all because I knew when I did, I had little control over them.

So, on the advice of a friend, I attended a seven-day intensive dog behaviour course with John Rogerson, who, if you didn't know, is considered by many to be the forefather of modern dog training. On this course I also met another dog trainer, David Davies, who would become my doggy guru and great friend too. The course changed everything for me and set me on a new path that I never knew existed. It was here I learned that I should play with my dogs if I wanted them to listen to me and want to be with me.

From that week on, I made sure that I was the one who provided the fun for my dogs and my clients' dogs when we were adventuring. I led the games we played.

Now, instead of messing about together, the dogs looked to me, the human, for play and entertainment. And because I had their attention, I had much more control. And more control meant they could enjoy even more off-leash exercise and freedom because I could get their focus quickly back on me whenever I wanted.

My story is not too dissimilar to what many pet dog owners have been through, and it may mirror your story too.

The consequences of allowing your dog to become too interested in anything else but you are exactly the same as they were for me. If you have spent a lot of time socialising your dog with other dogs, then that is something he will enjoy. Not only that, but he will remember that he enjoyed it, and he will seek out other dogs every time he gets the opportunity.

And that my friend is the 'lazy dog trainers' secret to success.

You need to play and interact with your dog more often.

You don't need a clicker, a whistle, a choke chain, a dog whisperer or a degree in canine psychology.

You just need to provide your dog with a reason to want to be with you.

'Play with your dog'.

If you can convince your dog that you control everything he needs to be happy, that's his food, toys and activities he enjoys, then you've got it licked.

To help you do that I have chosen to share with you the three most actionable exercises I know that will make living with your dog easier and more enjoyable, for both of you.

You can be a better owner, have a better dog, and you both can enjoy a happier life TODAY by implementing what's in this book.

I need to make a confession here, I've never been much of a scholar so putting this book together was a challenge for me. I hate anything that's too complicated, so we are going to keep things very straightforward. That way it is simple for you, simple for your dog and most importantly FUN for both of you!

Ready? Then, here we go!

But, before we start…

Dogs are truly amazing creatures. There are dogs who can care for disabled people 24 hours a day, service dogs who assist soldiers and police to find, apprehend and detain criminals and there are even dogs that with the power of their nose are learning to detect cancer in patients.

Unfortunately, there isn't a dog on this earth who can read (YET!)

So unless you have a dog trainer or some other support then anything you learn in this book you are going to have to implement. Happily for you, everything we are going to learn is free and easy, and all you need to commit is some time and energy.

Yes, this is the 'lazy dog owners' guide, but you still have to do some work…

YOU own your dog, so you need to take ownership of your dog and any problems you are having with him.

The good news is many of the everyday problems you are having are really easy to put right. For any serious problems you are having with your dog such as aggression you need to consult a professional dog trainer/behaviourist.

So let's do the work, together.

Let's take action now to change things and make living with a dog easier and much more enjoyable, and we are going to begin by me sharing the lazy dog owners first secret to success.

Chapter One

To be a best friend, you need to be the most fun!

A question for you. What makes your dog's tail wag? What makes him really happy? If he could write down the three things he loved doing most in the whole world how many times would you be on the list?

I have no scientific proof for this, but I'm pretty sure your dog doesn't lie in his bed at night plotting all of the awful things he is going to do the next day.

What I do know is most of what we term problem behaviours are just dogs doing what comes naturally to them, and in essence, they are just dogs being dogs!

Dogs need an outlet for the energy they wake up with every day, and the more you involve yourself with how your dog gets rid of that energy, the more he will look to you as a fun person to spend time with.

All dogs are different, and what breed of dog you own will play a big part in what they like to do. Almost all kinds of dogs like to do certain things, they like to play and exercise, they like to eat and chew stuff, and when they have done enough of the first two, then they like to sleep. If a dog gets the correct amount of exercise, then he will likely eat and sleep better also. Anyone with children will remember the Play, Eat, Sleep formula for a baby well it's not much different for dogs. How your dog gets that exercise and stimulation is all-important.

How do I know this?

When I started my dog adventure business, I thought it was enough to take the dogs in my charge for lots and lots of exercise so they would go home happy and tired. I managed this, but how they were getting tired was proving a big problem.

We used to walk or jog 8 or 9 miles every day with the dogs on lead and then when the dogs were off lead, I used to let them play together. They would run and chase each other, this would then escalate to play fighting, wrestling and mouthing each other. They were clearly having a marvellous time doing it, and they would go home tired and content.

The only problem was, they didn't take any notice of me at all! I had made myself an irrelevance to the having fun part of the dogs day.

If I were a parent, then I would have been the father who took them to the Fun Shack and let them run around like loonies for an hour and then take them home again afterwards. This may be good for tiredness and an occasional treat, but not great for improving long term good behaviour.

I could see this wasn't going to work long term, so I sought some help. The light bulb moment came on the John Rogerson Dog Behaviour Course I attended and where I learned that the more a dog owner did with their dog, the more the dog would look to them for stimulation and entertainment and so over time you would have a more attentive dog who enjoyed being with its owner.

Can't be that easy right? That's what I thought too, but what followed changed my business and my life, and it's changed the lives of our clients and their dogs too.

From that day on, I started doing stuff with my own and my client's dogs, playing, feeding, talking, grooming and all the while having fun. We made up find it and retrieving games, we also did some training but most of all I stopped them from playing with each other and instead all of the fun they had was coming directly from ME!

It was hard work at first, and I had to do some pretty stupid things to get my dogs to even look at me. But the more effort I put in, the more they responded, enjoyed what I did and saw me as a fun guy to be around

And guess what, I had more fun too!

This way of playing and interacting with your dog has many other benefits too. It means the dogs in our care are safer because they are near us because they want to be with us (and not any strange dog we might bump into on a walk.)

It's better for my clients too because they know that when they use our 'Play Together, Stay Together' formula for a contented dog then their dog will want to be with them when they take them to the park and NOT another dog!

To recap, if doing something with YOU is not two out of three on that list of things he likes doing then you need to stop your dog doing things you don't want him to do and make yourself more interesting to him. You need to be the thing that makes his tail wag.

But how do I do that I hear you cry!

Well, that leads us nicely onto step one of the lazy dog owners key to happiness.

Chapter Two

Step One – How to play your way to being your dog's best mate!

Dogs are naturally very playful animals, and the more we play with them, the more they will look to us for entertainment and enjoyment, and we become an integral part of their life.

If you have ever owned a puppy, then you know what I mean because trying to tire a puppy out can be haaaard work.

It seems as if puppies just want to play all the time, at least when they are not sleeping or eating! Whilst your puppy will hopefully naturally settle down as it matures, dogs never really lose the ability to play.

A playful dog is easier to wear out too. I remember years ago watching people throw the ball back and forth for their dogs and thinking gosh that must be so boring for the dog when in reality the dog had a job to do, it was getting rid of its energy and went home very happy.

A dog that loves bringing a ball or a frisbee back like this is dependent on its owner for entertainment so will look to its owner for it's fun and see them as their best friend.

Not all but many of the problem behaviours we see in dogs today stem from a dog just having too much pent-up energy or as we learned in part one from getting rid of that energy the wrong way. (For example, playing with other dogs!)

Do you think whilst you are out at work your dog really enjoys howling all day or chewing up your house? Of course he doesn't. That is often him being left with too much energy, and he is getting rid of that energy in a way he has learned while you weren't there.

To be totally honest, a normal on leash dog walk just won't cut it for most dogs anyway, and a half-hour on leash walk for a gundog or similar high energy dog is a bit of a warm-up really. The games I am going to show you how to play are high energy and will go a long way to getting rid of pent-up energy.

One of my earliest clients owned a six-month-old Cocker Spaniel (called Lily) who they were having recall problems with. We quickly found out that Lily liked chasing and sometimes bringing back a tennis ball that she had with her most of the day. We started by only letting Lily play with a ball when she was interacting with us.

Then using a long lead to control where she was able to go, we were able to play and interact with Lily.

Quite quickly, we were able to build a bond to the point where Lily looked to her owner as a fun person to be around, and the recall issues went away.

You can play almost anything with your dog. I've seen many dogs playing football with their owners. In fact, some have been so good they could probably get signed for Sunderland AFC! You can play with a tug toy, do some wild agility i.e. jumping over logs and benches in the park, play find it games, heelwork or clicker training, the list is endless, and so anything that involves your dog doing stuff with YOU is a good thing.

If your dog likes picking up plastic bottles, then just use that. I taught a pug to swim once by luring him with a feather he was playing with, so believe me this works!

Why use a toy and not food? Food is great. I love it and so do my dogs. By all means, you can use food to entertain and get your dog's attention and for some dogs who play too rough using a toy food maybe a better option. But what if you only teach using food and one day they are not hungry!

Playing a game with a toy is going to wear your dog out quicker than not doing so. That play helps build a bond between you and your dog and anyway playing is loads more fun than just shovelling food down your dog's throat.

To start, you want to keep it very simple for you and your dog. If it is easy and you both enjoy it, then you are much more likely to both want to do it again. Any game that puts the focus of your dog on you is going to start to build and strengthen the bond between you and put you on the way to having a true four-legged best friend. A simple retrieve and tuggy game is a great place to start.

Tuggy Tug Tug

Start this game somewhere with low distractions for your dog. Your front room or kitchen would be a great place for now. Get the tuggy toy out and twirl it around a bit, talk to your dog and in your squeakiest and most playful voice say 'Oooh what's this I have here isn't this a very special toy I wonder who would like to play with this with me.' Or words to that effect! Hopefully, your dog will have woken up by now will have cocked his head at you and be paying you some kind of interest.

Now make the toy move around the floor like a snake and encourage your dog to get the toy but don't let him have it just yet. We want to build up some desire and dogs are a bit like us in that they usually want stuff they can't have! Keep this up and when your dog is really interested in the toy or more importantly what YOU are doing with it let him have a sniff, then shake it in front of him and encourage him to hold it.

Once he holds it in his mouth, praise him with a 'GOOD BOY!' and have a little game of tuggy. Tug for a few seconds and then stop moving your arm, stand very still and wait until he lets go of the toy. And wait. When he eventually does let go reward him with the toy again. Repeat this five times and bingo you just taught your dog it is more fun to play with you than it is to play by himself with the toy.

This may take some doing but persevere. Keep the sessions quite short at first and try and end the game while your dog is still interested. Leave him wanting more. Do this a couple of times a day.

Once his tail is wagging, and we have a good drive for the game, you can begin to ask him to sit before you play tuggy. Then as he starts to really enjoy the game you can move to a different room to play, then your garden, then a quiet area of the park etc.

At each stage, you are teaching your dog that you are a fun person to be with.

Fetchy Fetch Fetch (I know, I have the best names for dog games don't I?)

One of the easiest ways to teach to retrieve is to have two identical toys your dog loves playing with. Get him interested in one of them, tease him a little as with the tuggy game and get him interested in the toy. When he is wagging his tail and wants the toy from you throw it a little way then when he goes to collect it, you then take the other toy out and start making a big fuss of the second toy.

Be enthusiastic, use a squeaky voice and generally be stupid! 'Ooh look what I've got isn't this a wonderful toy' etc. It may take a while, but as soon as your dog drops the first toy to investigate what you are doing, you throw the second toy for him, and you retrieve the first.

Keep this game going for a while and then start moving away from your dog when you retrieve the dropped toy. This will encourage him to follow you with his toy, then you can start throwing the second toy when he brings it closer.

I have made the instructions for these games very simple for a reason. What you achieve regarding the retrieve is of secondary importance to HOW you do it. If after a week your dog still isn't bringing the ball back very well but is wagging his tail and enjoying being with you then that is progress.

In fact, if you take two toys out and spend ten minutes throwing and your dog chases it, and you end up doing the retrieving, it's not the end of the world either. (In fact its good exercise for you too.) The start of everything is to get your dog's tail wagging and for him to enjoy and want to do stuff with you. Once you have that you can move onto some more formal training but for now just have fun.

TOP DOG TIP

We tease the dog a little to build up his motivation and drive for the toy. We want to involve ourselves in the fun and avoid just giving the dog the toy to play with on his own. Think of it as your toy you are sharing with your dog and when you are finished the game PUT THE TOYS AWAY till next time. One way to get your dog to think a toy is boring is to leave it lying around the house. Why do puppies always leave their own toys and pick up socks and shoes? It's because we make a big fuss and chase them around the house, so they think 'Wow this gets a reaction from my mam or dad!'

What to use?

There are some amazing dog toys on the market that are safe and durable enough to be tossed, chewed and tugged by even the toughest dogs, but you don't need to spend any money at all. For retrieving games, tennis balls are cheap as chips or a clean piece of hosepipe cut into 1ft lengths makes a perfect safe 'Stick' for your dog.

For tuggy games an old towel cut into strips and then knotted at each end will do the trick or if you are feeling handy and want something a bit more hardwearing, then a hard dog ball with a hole in it that you can push a bit of rope through to make a heavy-duty ball on a rope will make most dogs very happy.

Let's keep it even easier than that. Use what works for you and your dog. If your dog loves pinching socks, then make a tug toy out of some odd socks joined together. If he loves picking up plastic bottles, then attach one to a piece of cord and use that to interact with him. If you only let your dog enjoy that thing with you, then pretty quickly he will associate you with the fun, and once he does, you can play with any toy with him.

So there we have a couple of easy and fun ways you can begin to bond and tire your dog out quickly. You can and you should now play these games everywhere you take your dog. It's no good just playing in the house and letting him do what he wants in the park or retrieve only in your garden and letting him play with other dogs at the beach.

Although if you are still reading this, you are hopefully realising that allowing your dog to get most of his daily stimulation and happiness from another dog is not the best way to get him to bond and respond to you.

Play everywhere and your dog will want to be with you everywhere you go.

But I'm not always there I hear you say. I have to work; I have to take the kids to school and so on. Yes you do but now you have a way to play, bond with and tire your dog out when you are there.

This next chapter is going to explain how to keep your dog lazy focused on you outdoors, and keep him entertained (and out of trouble) when he's home alone, and you aren't even there.

I'm talking about how to 'Use Food'….

Chapter Three

Step Two - Throw away your dog's bowl!

No, I don't want you to start using a plate! Although I am talking about a big change in the way you view feeding your dog.

See, dogs were once upon a time scavengers and anyone whose dog has ever found a discarded pizza box in their local park will know exactly what I mean.

Yes, we have domesticated dogs now and not wolves but along the way we have without a doubt tried to make them fit into our human ways of eating meals.

Most pet dogs get a scoop of something twice a day with maybe a couple of biscuits as a treat.

Good enough, you might think? Well good enough to live on but not really very interesting for your dog I'm afraid.

If you own a dog and also work or even if you don't work, but your dog spends any time alone during the day, then you can definitely make better use of your dog's mealtimes and increase your dog's happiness by 150%. The answer is to throw away your dog's bowl and start feeding by hand or from a KONG, or another suitable food dispenser.

You can get more out of your dog's daily intake by spreading his food out into several portions, but don't start taking food away from your dog and putting him in a situation where he feels like he has to defend his food. Far better for your dog to see you as the giver of food and the provider of nice things that he likes, and leave any macho food-bowl standoffs for dog whisperers who enjoy being bitten.

So instead of giving your dog his whole breakfast or tea in one bowl, you could split it into five portions and use it as a reward for a simple recall exercise; you can put a small amount of food into your dog's bowl then walk away from him, and when he is finished, call him to you in a nice cheery voice and reward him with a handful of meal. Repeat this four or five times, always being sure to supplement the giving of the food with praise and affection.

I split my own dogs' daily ration of food and treats into thirds. One third is split between two small meals, one in the morning and one in the evening.

The second portion is spread throughout the day and fed by hand in various games and training exercises – some goes in my coat pocket to use when I'm at the park, and some is placed in a bowl that goes on my mantlepiece to use indoors either as part of training or just to reinforce any good behaviour my dogs might exhibit throughout the day.

The final third I use in food dispensers, which entertain my dogs throughout the day when I am busy doing other things. Depending on how busy I am, I may even split the whole day's ration so I train with half of it and the rest will go in food dispensing toys. I am going to go into the wonderful world of food dispensing toys next, but see how I use my dog's food throughout the whole day to train, entertain, and challenge him. Would your dog enjoy his food a little more if he has to earn it rather than just be given it as one or two meals to graze on whenever he pleases?

I wish I had discovered a KONG when my first two dogs were young. I cringe now when I think back to the damage caused by me not giving my dog something to do when I wasn't there. In our house, we had chewed banisters and door frames, the usual slippers, dog beds and even the T.V remote was destroyed by my Dogue de Bordeaux Barry.

Not content with one remote he promptly destroyed the replacement we had purchased at a cost of £50! (And yes, I did eventually learn the lesson that I shouldn't leave the remote where he could reach it or at least not leave The Jeremy Kyle show on when I went out!)

Munchy Munch Munch

The point to note here is dogs don't destroy things for the sake of it, but they do LOVE chewing and gnawing. If we give them something that they are allowed and encouraged to chew on and eat from, then they will be much happier.

If you didn't want to spend any money, then you could easily feed your dog out of a discarded and washed milk or orange carton by simply placing the dog's food inside and leaving the top off. The added bonus of this is that it's free, you are recycling something, and it doesn't matter if your dog rips it up as it was going in the bin anyway.

The downside to this is you really need to be there while your dog is eating from something like this as when they are finished the treats they may start eating the container!

So, in this instance, it's probably best to invest in a KONG or another kind of treat dispenser. They can be bought almost anywhere, they are not really expensive, and if you buy the correct kind, it will last forever.

They are also easily cleaned, and you can feed your dog's whole daily allowance of food and treats from them if you wish. The most important and useful thing about a treat-dispensing toy is it turns the mealtime into an activity for your dog, challenging them and gets them using their nose.

You can fill your dog's treat dispenser and leave it with your dog when you go out to work knowing that they are entertaining themselves by eating and chewing something safe and they will likely go to sleep once they have finished. In the puppy class we run, this is one of the ways we teach the puppies how to settle at home in a crate, so they don't develop any separation anxiety problems.

So giving your dog an outlet for his natural chewing and foraging instincts by feeding from a treat dispenser is an awesome thing to do for them. It takes a maximum of ten minutes to fill a few KONGs and if it saves you cleaning up chewed up Jimmy Choos or explaining to your neighbours why your dog was barking all day because he was bored at home then its ten minutes well spent.

You don't really have to throw away the dogs bowl either. Maybe feed one meal from a bowl and one from a treat dispenser or just feed your dog his treats from a treat dispenser. Once you start using one, you will likely use it more often. Do it. If he could your dog would thank you for it!

TOP DOG TIP

But I already own a KONG, and my dog doesn't use it? Well, try using it in the way I have described above and treat the KONG or other treat dispenser like you paid £100 for it. Don't leave it lying around once your dog has finished using it. Wash it and put it away till next time. If you treat it like an expensive pair of shoes you only use now and again then your dog will too, and he will look forward to the next time he gets it.

As with anything in this book, the more interesting you make it for your dog, the more interesting he will find it. So put some effort in and be creative with what you put in your treat dispenser. If you normally save your dog a little bit of meat from your dinner then stuff it in a treat dispenser instead of just giving it to him.

A treat given to a dog gives him a second of pleasure. Be creative with a treat dispenser, and you can give your dog ten minutes of pleasure with the same treat. You are making him work for his food, challenging him and getting him to use his nose too.

And speaking of your dog's snout, that leads me nicely onto step 3 of your lazy dog owners' FAST-TRACK' dog training degree… Your dog's scenting superpower.

Chapter Four

Step 3 - Unleash your dog's scenting superpower

Did you know that dogs are modern day X-men superheroes, and each breed has its own unique speciality?

Well, now you do!

There are lightning-fast Greyhounds that can race around a track at speeds of up to 40 mph; tenacious Terriers that will dig into a rabbit hole until you pull them out; scary-strong Staffies who can crush supposedly indestructible toys into tiny pieces; super swimmers like the Newfoundland that can glide through the water aided by their webbed feet, and crazy-intelligent Collies that seemingly work like remote-controlled dogs and can move a flock of sheep from one field to another.

But there is one superpower that all dogs share, and that is the gift of smell.

Dogs possess the same five senses as us: taste, touch, smell, hearing, and sight. But, it is estimated that 30% of a dog's brain is dedicated to analysing odour, which is 40 times larger than the area that our human brains dedicate to the same task. We know for a fact that a dog's nose contains around 300 million olfactory receptors compared to our measly six million.

There are dogs that can find a tiny piece of cannabis hidden inside a suitcase placed among 1000 other suitcases, and there are even dogs that are being trained to detect cancer in human beings. Medical detection dogs help alert people with diabetes when their blood sugar levels become low, which is a daily hazard for those with severe diabetes.

Now that kind of ability is not to be sniffed at…

This makes our dogs' noses around 1000 to 10,000 times better than ours, which pretty much makes your mutt an X-Dog. And a superpower like that needs careful control, otherwise your dog's nose will get him into all kinds of trouble, much like the children with superpowers in *X-Men: First Class.*

I'm sure you will be able to think of a few occasions where your dog's nose has landed him in some trouble in the past. Maybe he stole a chicken fresh out of the oven that was cooling on the top, or in the park he found a not quite empty but discarded pizza box and helped himself to what was left. He might, for example, be retrieving a ball one day when he suddenly drops it, stands stock-still and then whips his head to the left, and you both think 'Squirrel!'

We know that with all great superpowers comes great responsibility – the only difference with Spider-Man is it's your dog that has the superpower and you who has the responsibility for controlling it. Playing some nose games with your dog will teach him that he can use his powers and have fun with you. To paraphrase John Rogerson, we can say control the toy, control the game, control the nose, and control the dog!

You may be thinking that you can no more influence what your dog smells than you can control what he sees. Well, that may be true, but by playing nose games regularly, you can quickly begin to control what he enjoys smelling or finding.

Teaching a 'find it' (Or as I like to call it, Sniffy sniff sniff)

'Find it' is a brilliant game, and one I play with my dogs every single day, every walk even.

Don't worry if you think your dog can't find anything; just think of it as a slower and more civilised version of a retrieve, and you will understand how easy it is. The main thing to remember is you need to have something that your dog really wants to find, so if you're in the garden or further afield, I would use a number one or two item from your dog's toys or food Kryptonite. But as with all the games we teach, you are probably better off starting this game indoors where there are fewer distractions.

Show your dog the toy and make sure he is interested enough in it to actually want it. Keep the dog on lead to stop him from getting the toy straight away, and then you can place the toy somewhere really easy for him to find: behind a chair or cushion if you are in the house or behind a bench, tree, or bush if you are in the park. It doesn't matter if your dog sees where you put the toy at first, as he will still be using his nose. We want him to find it, remember? You need to make the finding of the toy very rewarding so he wants to do it again.

Then just encourage your dog to go and 'find it' and give him lots of praise and affection when he does. Repeat this four or five times until your dog has the idea. Then you can throw the toy behind a different thing, lead your dog a short way away from the area and then encourage him to go and find it again.

A huge mistake that almost all dog owners, including me, make with this game is that they rush ahead and try and make it too difficult by hiding the toy too far away. Then when the dog struggles to find the toy, the owner thinks he either doesn't like the game or isn't very good at it, neither of which is usually true. You are the teacher here; how fun and easy you make the finding of the toy or food will very much affect how enjoyable your dog finds the game, how quickly he learns to do it, and how much he wants to play in the future.

Find the food (Sniffy, munch, munch???)

You can play 'find it' using food as per the instructions above, and there are many other games you can play in the house that your dog will love playing, and you will enjoy watching him too.

You can use a baking tray or some plastic beakers to hide food under. Place five or so on the floor with a treat or some kibble under three of them, let your dog into the room, and encourage him to 'find the treats'. This is an incredibly simple game, but dogs love it, and you are encouraging your dog to use his nose.

You can start by placing a bit of food on the floor in your house. Let your dog see you do it, and then encourage him to get or 'Find it'. Repeat three or four times, and then place the food behind a door or cushion, and tell your dog to 'Find it', which he will quite easily. Once your dog has the idea, you can gradually make the game more difficult. You could play the game with food already in a KONG and hide the KONG. Then your dog has to find it and work to get the food out. This is double the challenge, double the stimulation, and double the fun.

You can take this even further by placing something tasty in a KONG, then wrapping the KONG in some paper, and placing it in a small cardboard box. Your dog then has to find the box, rip the parcel open, and remove the paper to get to the KONG and the food. My Barry loves playing this game and seems to enjoy ripping up the box as much as he does finding the chicken.

A lot of dog trainers get a bit snooty about using food to control your dog. They don't think we should be 'bribing' our dogs to do anything.

We have a name for those people, "idiots."

If your dog is food motivated, *and* he is difficult to control at the park, then you'd be pretty silly not to use food to keep him focused on you.

So, let's ignore the science speaking perfect dog professors who have all day to train their dogs.

You stick with these 'lazy dog training' techniques, and you'll have your dog eating out of the palm of your hand. In this case, literally eating out of your hand....

In conclusion

What to do next (and the day after that)

We've reached the end of this book, but this is just the beginning for you and your dog.

I often hear people say my dog means everything to me, but their actions don't really lead me to believe that to be true at all.

Yes, doggy cuddles are the absolute best, *but* I hope you can see your dog needs more than that to be truly happy and fulfilled.

So, if your dog means everything to you, then be everything to your dog. You have hopefully learned that it's not that hard to do.

If a lazy-ass dog trainer like me can do it with a few games, some enthusiasm and a handful of hotdogs (other treats are available), then YOU CAN TOO!

I've shown you three easy ways to implement changes you can make today to start and make your dog's life 100% more interesting and fulfilling.

Doing the three things in this book for just ten minutes a day will vastly improve the relationship between you and your dog, which will give you more control on your walks, and make off-leash exercise more enjoyable.

If you enjoyed this book then you'll LOVE my bestselling feature-length dog training bible 'How to Be Your Dog's

Superhero', and on the next page, I'll share with you a free chapter.

That's me done. Remember, be the owner your dog needs you to be!

Thanks for reading, stay lazy, and 'BE' the fun for your dog!

Introduction to How to Be Your Dog's Superhero

It's estimated there are around a half-billion dogs in the world (including strays) and nine million pet dogs in the UK. The World Canine Organisation (Fédération Cynologique Internationale) estimates there are 339 actual breeds of dog in the world today.

But did you know there are only two kinds of dog owners?

The first group has dogs that truly love them almost *all of the time.* They enjoy the company of their owners and tend to stay near them wherever they go. The next group has dogs who would often rather be anywhere else than with them and the further from the sofa they go, the less interested they seem to be in their human keeper.

Perhaps unsurprisingly, the owners in group one have dogs who hardly ever have any recall or reactivity problems. They take their dogs for stress-free daily walks anywhere they choose, they can enjoy a coffee or an ice cream at a cafe with their dogs, and when they can, they take their dogs on holiday with them.

The second group endures a different kind of dog-owning experience. When they go for a walk, their dog can usually be found in another part of the park altogether, where they may be eating poo, chasing pigeons, or more likely looking for and playing with their doggy friends. That's if their owners can find them at all. You see, while these dogs very much enjoy you whispering sweet nothings in their ear while you cuddle them on the couch, they quickly forget their name and often turn stone deaf as soon as you step outside your house. For the poor owners in group two, every trip to the park, beach, or woods has the potential to be a very stressful affair. They feel as if they are constantly telling the dog off for ignoring them, and it's a daily battle of wills.

The owners in group two don't love their dogs any less than the owners in the first group; they actually love them very much. But for some reason, the dogs don't feel the same way. There is a lack of connection; but how did this happen?

Getting a dog was supposed to be the thing that would complete your family and give you a reason to enjoy long relaxing walks in the park. This was the family member that would never grow up and leave home. So how did 'man's best friend' become 'that bloody dog' for so many of us?

Before we tackle that, I do have to ask: which category of owner do you fall into? Does your dog follow you around like you are the Pied Piper, or like many owners, do you have trouble getting his attention when he is sniffing a pee-covered lamp post, never mind when another dog appears?

What I'm really asking is: would you say your dog loves you and listens to you all the time? Or only when it suits him, and there is nothing else around that he finds more interesting?

If you are currently in group two, then don't worry, because I used to be too, and I know it wasn't much fun at all. In fact, it was a bloody nightmare. Yes, I too have stood alone in the park holding a dogless lead while I shouted for my dog to come back. He did eventually, but only when he had finished saying hello to every other dog he met.

I am going to show you how you can get your dog to listen to you and do what you want him to, even if at the moment, your dog would far rather chase something that has grabbed his attention. This superhuman power that you need to get your dog to look, listen, and pay attention to you can be described with another word.

The dirtiest word in dog training

I'm referring to the dreaded 'c' word. No..., not that one. I'm talking about 'control'. Having great control of your dog is something all dog owners should have, but it doesn't mean dominating your dog. It doesn't require you to shout at him or use an e-collar or a check chain. You don't need any of those things, but if you want to be a responsible dog owner, you bloody well do need to have very good control of your dog. Especially if you are exercising your dog off-leash, and yes, all dogs need off-leash exercise.

So, control is key. For one thing, the Dangerous Dogs Act (UK) demands you have great control over your dogs in public and private places. And there are hefty fines and possible prison sentences if your dog is deemed dangerously out-of-control.

The law is obviously important; however, the responsibility that dog owners have to their community and to future dog owners is equally important. As hard as it might seem to believe, not everyone in the world likes dogs, and people who don't like dogs certainly don't want dogs running up and bothering them. More out-of-control dogs will mean more dog-control orders and less public spaces to exercise and enjoy our dogs. And a world without dogs would be a very sad place indeed.

So now that we have got the 'c' word out of the way, and I'm warming to my task, why don't I shatter a few more myths about dogs – myths that seem to have wormed their way into the way we think about dogs? If you are very sensitive, then this will ruffle a few feathers, and by ruffle I mean pluck out and shred….

To get the full Prologue and introduction chapter of this book go to

www.mydogssuperhero.com/freechapter

Or you can get the full book from Amazon or Audible.

ABOUT THE AUTHOR

Dom Hodgson is an expert 'lazy' dog trainer, bestselling author and Europes leading pet business coach.

With his eldest son, Alex, he runs the UK's number-one dog adventure company, Pack Leader Dog Adventures. Since 2011, PLDA has been helping dog owners in Sunderland have more fun and less stress with their dogs.

In 2016, Dom wrote the bestselling *How To Be Your Dog's Superhero*, which is available to buy from Amazon Kindle, as an audiobook on Audible or you can get a signed copy (and a special free gift) by going to www.mydogssuperhero.com/getcopy . This was followed by *Walk Yourself Wealthy*, *Worry Free Walks* and *The Perfect Puppy Project, The Ultimate Pet Business Plan, and The Dog Owners Self-Isolation Survival Guide.*

Dom is an international speaker and teaches pet dog owners how to have more fun (and get more control) with their dogs, and pet business owners how to have more fun (and make more money) in their business.

As you know by now, Dom is lazy and has more than enough 'business' and 'busyness' in his life. He works with a small number of highly qualified clients and likes to spend most of his time writing or tending to his chickens at his home in Town Farm. Therefore, it's highly unlikely you will be able to tempt him to come and speak at an event of yours, or come and deliver a consultation. However, if you are feeling lucky, and would like to enquire, please email Beth on beth@packleaderdogadventures.co.uk , or go to www.growyourpetbusinessfast.com to find out more.

Dom lives in Town Farm with his wife Beth; youngest son, Toby; and their two dogs Sid the Cocker and Derek the Dogue de Bordeaux.

Other Books by the Author

All available from Amazon and Audible

Dog Training Books

How To Be Your Dog's Superhero: Transform your dastardly dog using the power of play.

The Dog Owners Self-Isolation Survival Guide - Discover how to quickly and easily exercise, entertain, and emotionally connect with your dog, from the seclusion of your sitting room.

Other Books in the Street-Smart Dog Training Series (1–3)

Worry Free Walks – How to transform your difficult, dangerous and devilish dog into a problem-free pooch you are proud to take to the park.

The Perfect Puppy Project– The ultimate no-mess, zero-stress, step-by-step guide to raising the perfect puppy.

The Hungry Games – Discover how you can bin the bowl and use food to play, train and entertain your perfect pet dog.

Pet Business Books

Walk Yourself Wealthy: The quick, easy and no-BS guide to transforming your passion for pooches into an insanely profitable and fun dog-walking empire .

The Ultimate Pet Business Plan: How to launch, grow and scale an outrageously profitable, impactful and fun pet business that dominates your local town.